Singing the Bones

Alexis Child

ISBN: 978-81-8253-870-2

First Edition: 2022
Rs. 200/-

Cover art:
Copyright Bob Veon, 2022.
You can find more of Bob Veon's artwork here:
https://www.deviantart.com/bobveon
Also, please visit Bob on Facebook:
https://www.facebook.com/bob.veon/

Cyberwit.net
HIG 45 Kaushambi Kunj, Kalindipuram
Allahabad - 211011 (U.P.) India
http://www.cyberwit.net
Tel: +(91) 9415091004
E-mail: info@cyberwit.net

Foreword to Singing the Bones -

This is the author's second collection of poems and a long-awaited wish come true. "Singing the Bones" is a searing collection of 65 poems of dark-hearted poetry that reaches out and grabs you by the throat with its tainted blend of truth.

Imagine human suffering like the torments of a haunted house and waning faith like collapsing stars. Envision candles that splutter to their death: This is a collection of desperate poems about the soul, the last reckless act, suicide, tears, pain and inner suffering like a dagger through the weakling heart.

In Alexis Child's second collection of poetry, "Singing the Bones" she opens with the prophet Ezekiel speaking a message of hope, but tells Jesus there is no more wine. It has run out. You will see glimpses of faith at times by the author although at the same time, she cries and dances with the devil with tears in her eyes.

Just sit back and relax and try not to hurt yourself. You are in for a real trick or treat. This collection of poetry touches upon horrific elements that are tense and those of the supernatural that terrify, yet you will also find that which is deeply profound; blessed are all that mourn you will read at the very end of the book.

In this book, "Singing the Bones" you will read of death in the romantic or gothic sense of the word and of that which is horrific. Yet, you will witness beauty as well in the innermost depths of the soul. These are bones that speak of hope and of horrors unimaginable and even warring psychosis. This is a poetry collection rich and just aching in emotion so prepare for the journey ahead. The author also portrays elements of the magical, fantastic and paints portraits of the surreal with vivid and emotive imagery. Expect to be held in the grips of both good and evil from which there is no escape.

For all those interested in that of horror and the supernatural, this book, "Singing the Bones" will provide the fear and chilling delights. It is for the older generation and even younger adults who appreciate all mortal terrors. Singing the Bones is for all who appreciate the sacred and the profane as well and is for anyone who has had a dark night of the soul. This collection of poems is guaranteed to enchant by the magic that can only be weaved by a dark priestess casting you under her spell.

The author of this book tells the reader they are blessed when they are at the end yet, cursed like a poorly created Ouija Board where the luck runs out. The bad breaks, the betrayals, all this tainted truth in "Singing the Bones" will take the reader to a place where they know they must be the first to explore it and suffer the terrible consequences!

Alexis Child's poetry and fiction has appeared numerous times on the web and in countless magazines.

IN MEMORY

ACKNOWLEGMENTS

This book is dedicated to the loving memory of my dear Mother, Dolores Belovich who was also a poet and musician and a great inspiration to me.

I would also like to dedicate this book to my Calico-Persian cat, Nefertiti; the very essence and song in my heart.

I also wish to thank Creepy Ghoul, Ferris and Andy Bones Fodero for all their love, help, and support in my life and for making this book possible. They have both been as a rock when the going got tough.

We sing the bones, as dear readers you will come to know of in this collection of sinister and macabre poetry.

My judgments go forth like lightning and you will be slain by the words of my mouth.

"Read this book with its terrible truths if you dare...

... As you would hold a map in your hands,

Running your skeletal fingers across the entire planet,

Whispering to the world,

Where does it hurt?

Where does it hurt?

Everywhere, everywhere."

EZEKIEL THE PROPHET -

Singing the Bones

Again he said unto me, Prophesy upon these bones, and say unto
them, O ye dry bones, hear the word of the LORD.

5 Thus saith the Lord GOD unto these bones; Behold, I will cause
breath to enter into you, and ye shall live:

6 And I will lay sinews upon you, and will bring up flesh upon
you, and cover you with skin, and put breath in you, and ye shall live;
and ye shall know that I am the LORD.

7 So I prophesied as I was commanded: and as I prophesied,
there was a noise, and behold a shaking, and the bones came together,
bone to his bone.

8 And when I beheld, lo, the sinews and the flesh came up upon
them, and the skin covered them above: but there was no breath in
them.

9 Then said he unto me, Prophesy unto the wind, prophesy, son
of man, and say to the wind, Thus saith the Lord GOD; Come from the
four winds, O breath, and breathe upon these slain, that they may live...

Contents

Fugue of Death

I am open to every agony
Flowing in prayer
Preserved in fire
Faced with the wrath of time
The hammer breaks the world
In pieces
Thoughts nailed firmly to the cross
Where nightfall is long

I die in the light
A Saint's mouth like blood
Dust-coated wings affect
My racing heart
In this mirror is Sunday
A time that it was time

The old year has gone to sleep
Creeping joyless hours
Pain speaks: perish!
Silence. Night. To prayer.
Something must happen.
Hissing. Wailing.
Here faces strange as animals

Maybe a black-haired poet going mad
As though it had run out of make-up
Your fallen world built on secrets
Dragged into the sunlight like vampires
I am bewildered

I claw at your hair, drink in your mouth
The reflection remains
The evil times from which my lips
Were made

'Of what do you speak?' dearest saviours
The evening hurls fiery embers from
Cold heavens
The earth is as bloody and bare as the
Body of our Lord groaning into extinction
Through pain, sorrow and loss
I bear the cross, I know the weight
I walk with thee amidst the flames
With curses, we are cast down upon the dust

Beautiful Nightmares

The ancient photographs are faded.
The home is lonesome and cold.
I confide to a flight of birds my
despair. In the twinkling of an eye,
you are gone. You must know you
are present at this burial now. The
candle flickers to its death. Sleep
beneath the stars in the blinking
twilight, beloved. Nothing is
forgotten in the book of eternal
meaning where a constellation is
like a day. Here heaven is no longer
blinded by dust.

An Angel Falls

Angel come. Whisper to me.
Come in the night. Elude
Your mystery. Let me inhale
Your emotions. Let me know
Your devotions. Break through
The gloom. Angel come. Angel go.
Invade this harrowing pain. Tears
In the rain. Come into the dark.
Wrap me in your arms. Bring us
Light. Angel come in the dark.
Fall away my heart.

Watching the black stars at
Night. To this day, a life of pain,
Loss and strife. You can't forget
The ancient scars of a day so
Long ago. In vain, I scream
In heaven's name. The devil
Takes my side. None can
Change this on earth or in space.
A demon loved the Angel. She
Was the white rose in the rain.
The salvation to his pain. The
Demon loved the angel back. But
She could never love him again.

Witch

Her eyes saw the stars,
Her hand held the cards,
Her mind learnt the meanings,
Her mouth spoke the words,
Her feet swept the ground,
Her nose smelled the incense,
Her skin felt the dim warmth of candles,
She left the ground,
Searching for stars,
And fell back to the flames,
Devouring her.

No Place for the Cross

In Golgotha, throne of bone, parched earth
spurned by the light of sun over ancient graves
of blood and moss, he rises like smoke from
the blood of the pierced. The wind summons
the gust of a stronger wind, whispering ashes
to scatter, raising a king from immortal bones.

Floating through the skull's jaw, he returns
to an empty Eden, capturing Heaven's tears,
gloomy before God, "This is not my world,
I was made for another."

Unwilling to give up his dust, he stares into
chaos, kissing wrath. Stealing earth's attic,
and light from the stars, he eclipses the angels
to seed a world unborn. He is suspended within
the womb of our awakening, and the matrix of
space in which there is no place for the cross.

The House With No Door

A world waits beneath the stone
Where death is a welcome guest
On familiar playing ground
Caretakers of carcass
Create their paradise of flesh

Gloomy horrors of the tomb
In my appointed rendezvous
With death plague me
I burn with mortal dread

What hidden terrors are in store?
Creeping outside the door
Making rasping calls
Haunting these unholy walls

Where fatal footsteps go
And curses lay the spirit low
On dim shores the echo
I must follow

The Sins of the Papyrus

She sits in church, cigarette aflame
Inhaling smoke, one drag
after the next
Calling his name.
A far off voice sounds in
the night
"Where is your shame?"

She takes another drag of her smoke,
Inhaling more carcinogen
Like little drops of water
are to dry bone
Pulsating blood and eyes,
Passing through a war.

No one knows her stories,
She is just passing through time
In exile,
And all her streets are written in dust
Like faded Egyptian Papyrus.

Katrina

Dear Katrina, it is the season/ I'm lucky I met you
I'm not sure how much of you I have discovered.
I tried to forget
But you grew roots around my ribcage
Just below my collarbones,
While the rest of you remains unknown.

The other day, I summoned the moon, music, and flowers,
and everything else I could think of
That would grab your lips and make them curve upward to smile.
I'm not good at writing poems about things that
have made my veins into a swimming pool
to backstroke through.
I'm not used to being as cold as this.

I know that it's hard to convince myself I am still
breathing, but let me put it this way,
You are Hurricane Katrina at lightning speed
Whipped wind, scraping at the bones, towards you
The walls, the floors, the slush that broke through
Yellow, with your name on it.
Now you will need to drag me off the wet floor
Still gasping for air.

We will slow dance in the living room and
We will not notice the windows rattling
But what you do not know is it sounds like a storm
inside you, where your heart remains.
I hear your name through the cracks in the doors

When the rain sets in with water snakes around my legs
That say forget-me-nots before losing became my loss
I was there in your forgetting until I was forgotten.

Hurricanes are awful
and I think you're more like the sound of the sky
when it plays games in the dying light.
In my Katrina, you are a wet and gorgeous disaster
So I need you to hold me like I am the only home
you do not want to destroy.

You see, after all these years,
I am still afraid of the unknown.
Applaud the moon, who steals the show,
And Sir, whoever wins the prize,
Do them justice in the skies.

Fire and Ice

A perfect utopia of happiness
Or a black ash-filled world
We will see as the days die
Night becoming the new normal
Some think tomorrow is now
And only darkness will reign
Like some sci-fi horror story
With us as the characters
All too soon to perish in vain
I do not look forward to that world
Where stars shine on in a night so black
In the end times, will we get out alive?
Will the day end in the night-time
Or will that day end in the day-time?
As judgment day unfurls over
Smothering fires of Armageddon
And there is only silence in space
In a world of raging hearts
And unfulfilled desires
Few would argue we are sublime
For denial, avarice and hatred
Are alive and well
And whether fire or ice, it can still be hell

Devoured

I am well acquainted with the wolf
Calling out in dead of night
It has been a year now
Protected by wild beasts
Or when everything went rotten,

Sanity was at the breaking point
Wounding the self and others
Torn viciously apart,
The wolves recognize the way they maim,

Poets began complaining
If blood I am, then what blood?
Easy for you to love your own kind
I, with eager eyes, am yearning and hungry,

I am the night
I am the day
You hear my call from far away,

Through flashes of temper,
Luna has lost her one and only love
A black massive cloud covers the moon's light
Blocking all the twinkling stars from our sight,

As far as desolation howls,
Once again upon the horizon, we prowl
We are devoured with savage greed and hate
Our bones are left to bleach upon the plains.

The Ghost of You

Both the weeping angels
And the weeping ghosts
Sang me a lullaby of sorrow
With rattling chains and wails
I found no comfort in their haunting
When faced with no tomorrows
Swathed in darkness and pain

Where phantoms glide in the abyss
Something much more sinister crept
With every morbid scream of fear
Where Beelzebub gloats on all misfortune
In the black light that keeps you
Awake at night

Between worlds, this trembling spirit
Was at war
Storm clouds announced an arrival
The path of my soul's demise
Haunted by someone still alive

Forgive or perish
Awakening to terror
In this horrifying house with no door
The house that stood empty
The house that depicted the end

And the ghosts are only as dead
As the ghosts within your head
Depart Seraphim and all of Satan's men
I should have loved a dead man instead

Dark Shadows

In the bloodthirsty heart
Of the night
We hear its screams
The vampire bats
Fly at dreams
Bleeding out into death
Until angels fall apart

In punishing light
Prayers of silence
Clamor in the night
In his tear-soaked name
Here, but now gone for eternity
Eyes open wide to cathedrals
As bewildered hollow bells

In the bitter ashes of Hades
I gave my life away
This crucified heaven
Maims and shames

You write my forgotten name
Like a cold black dream
Casting a spell over me
I walk with the undead
And I have never been
Loved this way before

You Must Be Certain of the Moonchild...

In the clear liquid
of a giant alchemical
flask, she is a hideous
form: a two-headed female
of gland secretions and
human blood in
the production of
the final mystic rite:
a Homunculi, the child
of my creation
The Devil's answer
to Eve where my
soul speaks to yours
through the Butterfly-Net—
earth beneath
the gallows, and my
artificial and living
self-sacrifice shall arise!
See me for the
monster and angel
I have become,
swaying beneath
the darkness and light
as I burn brightly on
the other side.

Dead Ink

I'm pleased as a murderer
Who has dealt his blow
Successfully.
As I walk in the gloomiest
Part of town-
Black as the grave
I wear the garb of the dead
For I have never really lived.

Was I being led by the devil
in this abode of human trash,
Vice, and crime?
Could he steal my soul?
And rob me of
My sordid mind?
Who caused me to fall
Into this trap?
A few steps more and
It's absinthe time.
Temptations of the soul,
My spirits revived.

I write a letter to the dead.
I write with a maddening hunger,
I write myself into nervous breakdowns.
Where the stars will not align,
And sadness is the sun.
Feel the shadows move across my skin,
Intoxicating, irreplaceable,

Magical,
You are all the above,
Guilty of sin and dust.

You wear a hellish guise,
Staring at me with open mouth,
Widened eyes,
You are the fight in my soul,
This life of crime,
The fight in my soul until the end
Of time,
This bittersweet pain is enough
To call your name and run for cover,
Demoniacal lover.

You are the hole down below,
You and I will make more dust.
Love me, love me
Put it in the ground,
Where the flowers grow,
In the silent hourglass of
The blackest hells that guide
Us now.

The Slumbering Host

I beg my tormentor, terrified
To lose my soul,
Then I utter my cry amongst
Monstrous shadows begging me,
To awaken.
The terror of dreams leaves
The eyes swollen and red while
I gasp for air.

I spiral down the bounding stairs,
And in fear, see myself
In this prison of agony.
The world is a prison of bars
Where I see myself,
Like a shivering star staring into
The pit.

The sweetest dream has stopped
My heart.
A figure approaches in the trees
White as a ghost,
Beckoning me to follow.
Follow me sister and taste
Of my shadow
I'll not let you go.

We walk hand in hand in the meadow
Now sing with me, he mocks,
Of death's dark chimes.

Live in a time better than God
In the dark and in the light.

We dimly hear the words:
No world is without big shadows,
I am the beauty and the malice,
Drink this poison from my chalice,
I give him my hand.

House of Dolls

I take my little dolls
Until I hardly recognize myself
I long for the world that
comes without pills

No bittersweet blanket of lies
Sheltering from oneself
The night, an open wound
Shakes and shivers
Calm your fears
Take your pills
The pendulum is
swinging, swinging

They prescribe pills to make you
smile at strangers
They prescribe pills to keep you
out of danger
They prescribe pills to keep the pain
at bay

Self-conscious about your weight?
Take a pill
Over anxious?
Take your pills
Severely depressed
Let's up the dosage
Pills that are the thick skull of everything

No matter how many drugs the doctors give
These pills aren't magic
I do not long for them
The doctors and shrinks
Cannot mold me
To fit into this broken society
So I can be 'normal'
So I can be happy

Take your pills
You're getting sick again
Go to therapy
Do I look sick?

Self-conscious about your weight?
Take a pill
Over anxious?
Take your pills
Severely depressed?
Let's up the dosage
Pills that are the thick skull of everything

No matter how many drugs the doctors give
These pills aren't magic
I do not long for them

The doctors and shrinks
Cannot mold me
To fit into this broken society
So I can be 'normal'
So I can be happy

Take your pills
You're getting sick again
Go to therapy
Do I look sick?
My mind is murky
Can you clear it, doc by Thursday?
I do not fathom how I survived
one more birthday

Why of course because of
Band-Aid solutions you give
To cure all my ills

More diseases doctor
Come along from pills
In the house of dolls
A medicinal death sentence
My journey will soon end

Doc you must be pleased you are fixing me
With drugs killing mind and body
At times I am not sure if I even know who I am____

Shadow on the Wall

Storm winds watch like death's strong birds.
I stand in the dusk, volcanoes lit up by fleeing
rivers full of blood. I toss my black head where
a hundred chains hang like skulls.

With blind anguish, I cannot name, I shield my own
lightness. I had long ago forgotten what home sounded like.
A golden, rusty candle gutters to its death. I am alone. You
speak a word that passes through summer and what I
dreamed feels its way into silence, dipped in the Son's blood.

Summoned to our end, a spirit among spirits is coming.
Its voice is a dim dungeon. Trembling like a star, I wanted
to look out. At midnight, a secret will arrive. But who can
comprehend it? Describe this web of love and hate.
None is wise, who has not known the darkness.

Damaged Goods

I hide in the shelter of a lonely life
Come choose your savage
Name any price

You could never love me
Because I live in lies
I come in a perfect package
With severed ties

In a sea of maddening sounds
For those not around
Broken is my happiness
At every chance I get

For years the floorboards
Creaked under a fearful self
Oh sweet devils, torment
Someone else

And then I'll ask myself
Why I feel so depressed

I am damaged goods
I'm misunderstood

I am damaged goods
I am damaged goods
To damaged gods
Even Jesus wept

Silent Things

Lost in the scheme of things
Promises hastily made, forgotten
Slivered reminders, shards of glass
Tarnished memories linger on

Letters the post never brings
A telephone caller failing to ring
An unreliable world of offbeat timing
Distractions prevail and dreamers despair

Their longings unabated
The decisive hesitate
Tainted by remnants of a history
Whose securities ceased

Hope delivers prayer to sedate
Until the promise arrives
The entombed have reason
To believe assured of silent things

Back to the Asylum

Swimming up from the bottom
Of a black sleep
Nightmare tumbles out
Into still morning
The Narcissist King
Remains on his throne
Outside, the wind screams
Howling like a dog

Your big brown eyes
Are everywhere
Teeth gleaming
Like tombstones
Chill grips my heart
With mortal ache
My past hangs in the room
As a thick cloud
Heavy shapes lean over me
Like nurses attending to the infirmed
You were just the sort of drug
I would invent

A windowless corridor of pain
Threatens to shut me in again
Memories circle empty air
Sliding down my back
Like a cold draft
As summer ends

A fog of echoes
And I am caught
We are astronauts
Asleep in the sea
The home will weep
With evil's frown

Not One of Us

Pain trickles through my
Fingers like water
Menacing witches float downwards
In this new earth of emptiness
It rains and the wind is never weary
Clinging to a moldering past
There is a roaring noise to
The whispers I hear inside
Locked doors, rats and angels
In the attic of melting mind

Every atom of blood
Which would you curse?
I must be dreaming
Something supernatural
The moon howls back
Lonely and black
I sit with you under the dry earth
The chrysalis opens
Your image flickers in the dark
I try to hold this lifeless ghost
You are so distant, yet so close

I spread my melancholy like dandelions
In one quick whisper of a breath
No longer will it take from me
I have decided to let go of my slow death
The pain of growth
The beauty of letting go

This redemption
Let it pour now
Let it rain
For evil lives all around
Let it rain more for our sorrow
And these flames that waste away

The wind is mournful
Like slithering shadows across the room
Chilled fingers creep across the glass
Living within us now as a dying god
Gather them up like sleeping flowers
Where all the forgotten children go to
Mourn their solitude
And conversations with the past

Hymn to Him

You were the sun that burnt my skin
Until silence was all that stirred
The moon's long gone home
All the stars are fully grown
When I no longer say these words
I'll give them to the wind, the birds
The trees so that they will still be heard
And I will no longer be alone

Strange News from another Star

Troubled warnings shriek in the night
Unutterable things in mystical power
Blighted by a celestial nightmare
On ominous shores
The departure of the strange miracles
That shone so lovely in the sky like Orion
Retreat like raptures in the stars
Now cold in raven's claws

The liquid mind dreams of the moon
Dancing in the night
Veiled by demoniac clouds
Speak to us, sweet Sorceress
And our mournful spirits
Will go beyond a funeral march
To the grave

The last fatal kiss in cold black days
Is like a crawling spider in the crying rain
Searching for things you dare not name
The sun and its death burst into flames
The night opens its eyes to a night palace
Where there exists a solemn hymn in the wind
Sorrow is the dying years
In our raw and bloodless hearts

In exile, the living skeletons remain
The living dead
In the cradle of despair

The piano plays in an empty room
On the canvas of our soul's depths
Destined star, oh mirror…despair, calm
Distant like a celestial dream, so afar

Pale warriors, bittersweet is the mouth
Of memories where the shadowed
Chariot takes us
You carry fear as a savior
If one day your bed becomes a grave
Will your thoughts fade away?
Will injustice disappear?
Will the gods perish?
Who will stop the rain?

Ghost Dance

Voices invade my sanctuary
A conspirator's wicked laugh
Imbues the noise of industry
Exploitation of needs
The blood red sun assaults my eyes
Apocryphal sights I can see

From my room as curtains rise
Upon the foolish specter
This misery
Money maker's prize

The stone angel forsakes his tool
Becoming the blood letter
A cold convenience
Captivity rules

Dogs bark, engines drone
Architects rape the land
People move faster
Robot bodies, servile minds

Determine their existence by machine
A mission is mistaken
Purposes are bastardized
Hark! The fall of humanity

Will my strength return
In this slow suicide?

In this combat with death
What is my prize?

Ghosts dance in detonation zone
Cheek to cheek with paper dolls
Ancient native spirits moan

Life is locked inside a wall of sound
The maker laments the torpor
Thick and trappings tall
Wanderers of the wasteland seek
Soul asylum

But where is home?

Death, be proud

Through cursed-like lips
Melancholy reigns as
Butterflies fly away
My flesh is of a church
Where none will pray

You look like the moon
As you say goodbye
Welcoming home
The cycle of the living
And the dying
In love's resting place
All the friends we've left behind

I shiver in solitude like
A granite tomb
Singing songs in lament
My memories are of you
In sorrow, a broken
And cracked bell
The dark sorcerer weaves a spell
In my blind bed

Infernal, eternal eyes
Never sleep, never dry
A Phoenix rises extinguishing
Itself by fire
Enchanted, enthroned by the Nile
We let you go to the dance of the stars

And the planets
We let you go into the wind's breath
And the hands of the star maker

Am I a lover, a sinner brooding on
The world?
The blind-hearted phantom
Terrified of pain
To pleasure flees
In the mouths of the four oceans
I seek the beyond in the heart of life
The Sphinx unfurls her wings
Eternal and free
I drink from the silent river
And wear the mark of a Queen

You wrap your arms around me
And whisper to me of myself
I can still see you sleeping
Like thunder when it rains
As death comes to meet me
It will lie in your eyes
Where our hearts will once
More sing free of desolation

Mithridatization

Will I dissipate in the dark until every
Trace of me fades, discarded and desolate?
I am a sister of smoked glass
Whose blood is black and cracked silver
My mother rises from ashes out of her clothes
She wishes me not to join her
Retreating back into this world's end
Effortlessly like a cart of dead flowers
After unhallowed eternities hiding in my skin
Only another could unmake and undress my spirit
I must give what I most desire
I become one with the opiated dream
A dead palm that can no longer wave its fingers
Some grow backwards backlit in an apothecary jar
Sleepwalking and somnambulistic
By the blackout of knives
Where are their screams now?
The black dog on my back
Induces the sensation of liquid filled lungs
Drowning skies
Some do not return at all
Living with ghosts demands
Utmost solitude and vigilance

Singing the Bones

Under my skin
A fire burns without a smile
Under my skin
The strangers are not
Welcome here
Under my skin
I look longingly at
What powers are
In his spirit

Under my skin
All locks are one in
A square glass box
A crack opens the sky
From the dead
To the living
There is the Kingdom of God
Under my skin
Our bodies are like castles and
Battlefields in blood
We do not know what to trust

There's a gypsy wearing black and a lover
Wearing white singing bones
With fire in the night
Under my skin
One of them was born with poems
In her mouth

Making holy what she touches
And what touches her

The moon surrenders to us
Will you travel with me?
Under my skin
All loves pale beyond this sacred one
The burial has ended
The soul's language understood
A prayer to travelers after
I bare my heart before the throne
Singing the bones together

Song of the Blind

The flames whisper
Feeding my corpse with fire
Horror to the light that laughs
Timid eyes look far
Amongst stars and ages
Shining like vivid sword
Murmuring a mystic world
Phantom wings of night brood
Virtuous and vicious
Earth too is lonely and old
A nightmare of unutterable things
We look upon your face
The torn breast of night
A distant bell, void and null
I am mothered of a muse
Invisible as the grasp of fate
O' Mother of melancholy
Shattered, you and I are one
Only the child is soft with flowers
Deathless and divine

Garden of Indolence

Stygian winter of cold shadows,
Do away with your mocking gaze.
Infuse me with hues of sadness,
Overcast skies, black as marble
Tombstones. Infernal hope, depart!
Despair return. Sorrow is wiser,
And more constant. Leave all
Behind that makes indolent
Dreamers, fools of us all.

Apostle of Infinite Space

Lunar God, curse me not,
Of new and cherished memories
in my heart. Be not a stranger
to our fate.

Prince of Spheres,
Bow before Hecate—
Come unto me
through the golden gates.

Rise, chosen priest!
Secret eternal flame.
Scribe, what magic is
created: The Book of
the Law and its 3 grades,

Man of earth and of
Elysium's grace.
Be not a stranger to our fate.

Shadow Keeper

In the spiritual dawn,
Sadness and madness reside
And cunningly conspire
Like nails that hammer down,
In the crying rain,
To swallow the sky,
Where dreams are like glass,

Deep in space under starless
Nights, these obsidian eyes
Fathomless seas are like a
Bewildering world waiting
Beneath the skin
Of fairy tales and fears,

Galaxies and lonely stars
Are like ghosts speaking
In tongues. Earth is but
Hell's heartbeat, a long-
Forgotten cemetery

It is I you have been
Looking for that goes
With you everywhere
Like a shadow or friend,

At your word, we sleep in
Silence and no longer open
Our mouths at Heaven's door.

In the ghostly darkness,
Awaken the dreamer
To the saintly ecstasies,
O' irreverent world.
I have always believed
For bigger things.

Victoria

The crazy burden
Everyone knew about
They loved the thin, happy kid
Vicky is hugging her knees
Arguments in the background
Someone is with her

White with panic
Her face on the ceiling
It doesn't seem right to cry
Cupping her ears
like tiny seashells
A calmer sea
Not the woman in the ambulance

Washed up like an old bone
She opens to the sea
Black, shadowy mouthfuls
A silent, hate writhes in wounds
One cannot communicate
Whir in ill wind of lapis lazuli sea
She claws her way towards the heavens

Staring corpse-like at the ceiling
Someone had saved her again
So many piles of pills, the razors,
the bottles, the blackouts
More ambulances than city hospitals
Therapists and Psychiatrists that just

gave up trying
And all the sideway glances
One could ever hope to recover from

She is smiling diabolical and tragic
Stupidly and sorrowfully
The world still black as a riddle
Suffering a fine madness
Victoria is not Victoria anymore

Just a roaring sea of words
Like witch's curses
For drowning lungs
She no longer sees ghosts anymore
Afraid of herself
Trauma, that mother you live with
Has many faces you discover like no other
You were lucky this time
But even still are gasping for air

Tell Me a Ghost Story...

Feast on my magical blood
Join me in the forbidden forest
Created from sleepwalking and nightmares
Conjure up the ghosts
Raise the dead and the fear to life
The overflowing milk
In December's dismal light,

The dangerous face in the window
Something outside in the dark waiting
Send it back to the terrible tomb
Crumbling in silence to dust and decay
Awake from your silence
For freedom and life
Conquer that Isle long forgotten!

We are the creators of ghosts
And monsters
Never free of the horrors
The shape of our fears bring us to our death
Mad love between the dog and the devil
The evil prevails that lives inside our mind
Battling the demons of darkness
For just one more night
But the demons made us believe
They knew what was best
Cutting the heart right out of our chest,

And the wind with the wolf's head
Howls at the bridge
Hiding in shadow
This is the devil's allegiance
Follow the bones,

Dance on the courageous backs
of the broken
Only they can be trusted
Beyond this sound of distant thunder,

The vanished smile of days
Our grieving in vain
Skeleton fingers drop over
The moon's pale beam
Mourning over a dreamless sleep,

Warring psychosis. Go into night.
Preserve me in myself in this hazardous
Fragment of a face,
These ashes laid to rest with great
Solemnity!

First Star I See Tonight

The sun sleeps
The moon weeps
In the cracked sky
Drowning and funerary

Angels and Gods fall
Like raindrops
In the dark sea
And that's what brings you
Closer to me

You kiss these lips
And offer a tantalizing smile
I'm taking off my armor
Captured by your irresistible charms

As you move sensuously over
My cold flesh
I die in your arms
And that's a sweet, sweet death

This could be heaven
This could be hell
In our devilish and
Mysterious realm

Your touch destroys my army
I've loosed the ghoul
The demon that wants only you

You look beyond all my imperfect scars
We live on a different star

Murderer

Who entered the door?
When I had the key?
I remember forgetting
Hands passing right through me,

Over my skin and closed throat
I was diminished of my own accord
The smell akin to fear, rotting leaves
Blow in through an open window,

The house was rotting
The lights stayed on while we slept,
A strange film like wax hung over me
In the collapse of the wreckage,

How little I understood
Like a black-and-white photograph
In the bloody aftermath,

You are gone
Key marks scratch the door jamb
The paper lamp sweeps the remains
Of what was obvious and what was lost
Night seeps through the window
As a warning in this bloody holocaust,

The final maelstrom covers the cursed night
Morning never arrives peacefully from the final fight

With soft red flesh as red soup again and again
Your cold eye stares at me through paper skin,

You died so young, oh so young
Why did I deserve to live?
My guilty confession unuttered?

I was always the invisible one
Walking like a spirit amongst others
They would hurt me just for fun
But no one expected me to become a cold-blooded MuRdErEr...

The murders started slowly
Each night, another would be gone
You could call this unholy
But when being a MuRdErEr, splatter doesn't matter...

Devil's Bones

Dressed in black
with a spirit to match
the moon chases the sun
An eclipse on a fateful day
every few years
and pulls her down into a deep
Dark onyx hole
she's climbed out of before
She tries to outrun the past
She's tried to run fast
but the demons are faster

Scarlet Heart

The future is red fluids
Seething with rage
The night is dead and long
She wonders why she is
The only one breathing

On this dark-eyed Halloween
She can hear their voices
Dismantling her
One bone at a time

Her breath is tangled in a whirling
Dervish of words
Making her pale skin in a black dress
Look like a painting

They sway together in the wind
Branches tangled and twisted together
Until they could not ignore the nothingness

She wrote a poem
The very last one
And then put down her pen
And wrote the last sentence
"I saw death and it was beautiful"
How odd to ignore the memory!

And then that very evening
Where a small dream hides

She fell into a dark trance
Like the subtle scent of frankincense

In remembrance of princes and pain
She shuts her lovely and childish eyes
Scorned by the dead light

The moon no longer beams
In chaotic night
And the stars never test the extremes
Of a heart sinking into the sky

The Devils You Know

The stars hang low
Fulfilling a prophecy
Asking me to accept what I cannot
The marble in these digested eyes
Looks through eclipsed sunsets
Leaving them bewildered and stuck
On this fretful journey to forget

The wolves in the night find me
In perilous night
This home is cursed by ghosts
Without names
My mother would say I was a flower
That grew without any light

I am a haunted house
Where I choke on the ashes
Of shame and regret
I drink from the poisonous cup
Of madness
Besieged and tortured
By hideous devils
I am versed in pain
Secret sins in the cold light
Of day

There are eerie halls
Blood-stained walls
In a house with no windows

In a house that's now yours
I died a long time ago
In this room with no doors

The ghosts move to and fro
Across the floors
Where I lived and perished
The specters feed my agony
As a vast and unseen galaxy
No one dares enter the home
Where the windows
Are forgotten songs

The lunatic knows all
Like a silent god
An evil sorceress laughs
Touching what belongs
To the underworld
Seeing more devils
In the shadows than
Hell could hold

Alone

The raging wind is a
Brutal force where
The spirit goes
There's no better reason
Now than to lock the doors
The windows
I have been caught dead with
My spirit within my hand

I am a pale ghost
Lost, wandering
Chasing whims and shadows
Hiding in dark places
Now free of tooth and flesh
Everything I once imagined

I reach with no arms
And stand with no legs
I am the breeze you feel
On windless nights
That will take away your breath

I watch with no eyes
And listen with no ears
I am just the shadow
Cast still within that of yours

To most, I am faceless, nameless
And bear no threat

In the distance just a silhouette
That no one notices
A ghost you know exists but don't believe
A ghost that haunts itself in this dark dream
Say you'll remember me

Darkest Dreaming

The room hisses at me
In a room full of stars
Intoxicated with sweet madness
The bells will not die down for me
Nightfall is long

I will sing to you of this triple-headed
Skull that scatters death to the four corners
We will have our supper and play in the fields
Until there is moonlight on roses
In an innocent wasteland

There we will know our mother's love
And tomorrow know no creeping, joyless hours
The oracle foretells a song of deepest dying
Let me swim to your depths

The Vanishing

Through closed eyes,
the merciless wind brings
the quivering branches that
love me not.

You blow into my hair
in deepest night where
shadows stand at my side;
They are present at this
burial.

This mortal enemy
Mourns under the cold
light of the moon.

In this dying day, we cry
out in the world in search
of certainty. In a dreadfully
forsaken voice,

The piano plays in an
empty room.
Are you not afraid of
this cold star?

This Night Has a Thousand Eyes

The lost man unlearns his past
Strange and damp beneath the tomb
Take cover! The evil was good
Strange and luminous among the grave
The devil is dying
Bizarre! You feel quiet witches below the sky

Escape! The evil will be born
Weird and desirous beside the flowers
Repent! The end is fleeing
So scared before the sky
Beware! There are colorful ghosts over the mist

The insanity will die
Sinful and huge before the spirits
Poisoned under the shadows
I taste scary Shivas among the gods
Alack! The demon has vanished
Beware! The day shall flee

You stroke sensuous ghouls above the gods
The Queen will vanish
Trusting, hopeful
Fading slowly, no words left

Where in the end
The face in your mirror
Forgets to go home
When the world was new

Death Watch

I have grown weary of the day
The evening draws near
With death as a glimmer in my eye
Drink from sorrow
The well is filled with dread

The fields darken
The home is lonesome
I sit silent before the lamp
I rant and write a poem
No friends are visible anymore

The hour sinks in alien night
The sky falls down inside us
Like malignant poison
The shadows shimmer 'never ever'
We look deep in the stillness
The soft light descends into me
As a dark dream

The Ninth Hour

You stare out of the mirror
Spiders lurk cursed like you
A flame of suffering
Your flame of woe
Adorned with a crown of thorns

What pale-blooded beauty
Who before was treated
Badly nods on the cross

The scorn of mockers darkens
Who looked upon you
A shadow hovers
Where no one hears screams

For you it is always night
Stabbing your white, desolate eyes
Like spears in evening clouds
Keeping order with angry, shaking fists
Heavy and disturbed, you live on trembling

You summon your hosts who console
Despite the evil times
But weeping for fate
There faithless tombs
Dream in blood
Where in Hell deception dwells

Ultima Mortis

I throw her to the water's edge,
cover her with stones.
I regret, but then forget
her cold beauty that carried me away,
where the sun now sleeps completely.

An evil conscience of glory and relief
makes me think the Devil is the master
of this skill.
How lovely she is on a bed of flowers.
There is a morbid charm where a sob
escapes under frothy blood.

My soul trembles on the banks of death,
where she is swept away,
Far from the sight of God
there is still a guilty desire
for the laughter of the sea,
those poisonous eyes
breathing life into me.

A scarlet tear runs from her cheek.
This is goodbye.
The crooked shadows look down with
shame to wake the dead.
Heaven and Hell collide.
Please don't be dead.
Just one more miracle?

Drowning in her panicky moans,
I realized I was indeed, a ghost,
watching the night sky made up of bones.

The Jesus Jar

I am fragile, beautiful and dainty
as a diamond as I slice through thick
glass. In these dangerously troubled
waters, the ghosts of my life are wilder
than the wind. My bedeviled mind isn't
strong enough to fight them. Crying for
liberty and peace with trembling hands,
the Jesus Jar is empty. Bring me a torch,
blessed by the Angels. I descend
so low that I am like a dream forgotten.
I fall, I fall to despair. I hide in the vast
Hell of shadows. I cling to hope in starless
sky.

In the maze of savage fate, we have come
here to free ourselves in the dance. Shall we
at long last find a safe and serene haven?
Shall we stop the roaring thunder where
curses are doubled during the night?
I am disappearing inch by inch into this
house. I leave the dead at my doorstep
and all their dry bones. Deliver me,
promised land of Zion!

Dialogue Between God and the Ghost

Where we lie in our shadowy tomb,
numb as a fossil, night arrives closing
doors with little sighs, starless and
motherless. Fleeing through my fingers,
I am bled white, most devout with quick
hands like spiders in the ocean of the soul.
I cast off my identity. Blank as when I was
born, Sunday's ghost cannot rest seeking
dead men's cries.

The hunter appears clothed in the skin
of his kill, corpse-white, walking after
other gods of which he knows not. Burning
incense as an offering to Baal, the leprous
chatter and angels fall like rain. No miracles
exist in a dead lover's eye. Grief has an honest
grimace, blackening flesh to bone, flowering
and devouring me.

Heaven's Orchestra

A fallen star is a fallen star,
We can think ourselves into
Anything at all,
The sins of the wicked and
All their misdeeds,
The heads of saints and the
Blood of Jesus,

A Shaman's smoke will lead
You here,
To all the lies of the human heart,
More constant than the constellations
And all their courses,

I am older now and scarred enough
To wake the dead,
And when my sad and tired life
Has expired,
You know I've made my bed
With the taste of holy death,

Call me a constellation,
As bright stars burn out,
When the moon and stars have
Lost their song,
Yet when I hear the angels
Singing they make music
In the human heart.

Moon Dance

I move inside this mood by
command of the moon
I move in solitude until my
face is lost in the mirror
My mind has made promises
to heal
I move sideways and upside down
with fire and smoke
Only a Shaman could seek his
wisdom here
As a woman of sorrow like a broken bell
I walk in solitary places in secrets and sobs
I await the true self
inert as a rock

Whispering Stars

The stars never tell secrets
Or words themselves would freeze
The inner world breaks down
And night never sleeps
Everything is bending in one direction
My eyes sharpen the sky
Until I can return to my own dark planet
With sacred words, gifts of ancient madness
But my face is moon-white frailly singing
To heaven in a spiritless room
I am waiting on an angel to take me home
I speak kindly to strangers
I don't wish to go alone
Orphaned and lost

I wear my painted face like a saint
With these bones out of place
I hold my hands up to heaven
And swallow black stars
Spitting on silence
Cautious not to confess all
On my blind journey
Daylight is stern and tearful
Without shadows to hide me away
I can only see the light with one stone eye
I call your name, star-bright and tongue-tied
My liquid mind is filled with peace
We glitter like dust on timeless shores of eternity
Celestial wings embrace us close
Your surreal lips guide me home

The Starry Midnight Whispers

Stars, bright hope of man's desire
And the man in the moon looking at me
In which one reads his blessing or his curse
Tell the baby when he awakes
To watch for my return
It is a bitter time of year
When your light begins to burn
And you depart dispassionately
Leaving a desert sky
The night has many eyes
When the bright sun dies
For every star a million fall
When you look coldly into my eyes

You are Orion to me glittering
How beautiful you are
Although you have flown away
Like hope by night and by day
Love is unseen by the naked eye
In the heaven of our song
This passion will no longer penetrate
Your smile is chilly under this vault of hell
My spirit struggles in the shadowy light
Under the dark night of your spell
The stars and moon doubt from now on
They could ever dwell in the realms of day
For those born in endless night where you remain

Love and Death

I witnessed the moon, the stars, Jupiter
And Mars collide in your glance
Until the blood ran dry in the dance
Never to glow with silver rapture
A single smoked tear will not change
Your mind, a city's death by fire,

We closed our eyes like tigers
In chaotic night
Talking to strangers
Drifting, falling
Through ice and inferno
When the war of the beasts
Brought about the world's end,

Dark Sorcerer, I boldly stand
In heaven's eye
Yet I still see what is left of the sky
All of this just to erase you
From my mind,

And from the face of every mirror
We pass into the past of razor-sharp
Orbits. Under a scythed moon
To love is a curse, this gloom acute
Under shadow's wings,

In prophecy, heavy rain and beyond
It was as if no angel dared to breathe

For this time prepared
Close the lid, drive in the nails
Do not forget the wind that longs
For your skin, hero of the dawn
I have waited for too long...
I believe that this is my greatest hour.

The Cracked Bell

In grey curse I grieve these
empty hands
I am filled with such great death
I understand nothing
I close like flowers
towards evening
Abandoned like fallen rain
Stars that fall to their knees
The cracked bell chimes

In deserted town
I praise monstrous and deadly things
In star and storm
My nature is discord
Darkness separates me from all men
Transformed into cruel wind
I am entangled in a stricken moment
of my fall
The dead church builds scars from stones
As one who never slept again

I am stamped into dust
In this night's dead eyes
My feet remain nowhere
With no steps leading to the church
of great suffering
The bells die for me
in wind of my prayers
Invoking God in vain
No night for me

Kissing the Corpse Goodbye

The mad magician never leaves
He is the breath in my lungs
The taste on my tongue
He is my skin and my within
Everywhere I've been
Everything I've seen
He has crafted me in his furnace

The sickness churns my stomach
Like razor blades
He knows of my weakness and
I cannot break free of his spell
When the cold winds blow
I know this fear more than most
I am even sought out by mortals
Who bled my skin
There is no sanctuary in hell

I sought out a safer place to hide my soul
Where no one goes but ancient gypsies
Not even the Magician of the dark arts
and great sin can find me here
There is a forest where no fire burns
The sun is not too bright
The branches are long and wide that hide the sky
It's thorns can tear anyone from limb to limb
Setting wicked traps

This is the Black Forest
That can entrap and ensnare

Some have fallen into sand and cannot breathe the air
The demon's chorus can be heard here
I am the keeper of others' fate
I am shaking the devil off
Here I am omnipotent. Magic girl
I whirl and spin - shake shake shake

When my methods become tried and tested
I turn to the loving gypsy folk
Vanquishing all my foes with toothless grins
And chocolate eyes, holes on their soles
They wander but do the impossible if you trust
My spirit is at rest in the Black Forest
Following the stars, the fortunes
My altered circumstance

I met a gypsy woman while dancing
Under the light of the moon
Who spoke old wisdom
To snare a husband
I ask her crystal ball eyes about my past
She just questions my future
It no longer looks scary

I can finally whisper home on the open road
I have lined my pockets with fairy dust
Just in case
Superstitions keep the long, dark shadows at bay
The closet skeletons that kissed me have died today
Now Babylon may pray
I found the Keys to St. Peter
It's just another day

A Country Far Away

The drowned skull of the night
Answers quickly weeping all the time alone
Tell me you are missing me
I want to be with you

Come here with courage
Arrive by means of scents
Or I shall be gone before you come

Promise me sandwiches, sweets
And the heads of old saints
Madcap lover
I'll be kissing you like a thief

Your dark eyes and hair
Scatters everywhere
Your crazy laugh teases me
In the lovely forest with blue air

Under the whispering grasses
We'll take the pale road
There is a secret window
Smiling in there

Blood at First Sight

I am a shadow in the blackest night
A whisper in the light
The wind no longer walks
In my hair
A cold fire snaps at my skin
In the approaching dawn
Drained mercilessly
From one dark night of passion

Yet if only suddenly she would live
I would consume her again
Like a cheap wine
Swooning under her powers
I hunger, but never again wish to drink
This romantic desire lingers

Let me walk you through the dangers
Of kissing the necks of strangers
Hear the darkness all around
How to cry without a sound
A very sad affair

The moon remembers the ecstasy
Of her sweet body
I am weeping with tears of blood
Even as the darkness comes
I cannot drown this pulsing dream
Where each day the sun will burn
A little bit brighter

"Make me into you"
I can sometimes hear her plead
As passion holds sway
Perhaps I've even begun to hallucinate
And feel a pain that isn't even mine

Tales foretell her demonic apparition
Is somewhere yet unknown
Perhaps in graveyards at midnight she roams
Where men become lost and disappear

Take heed fearless creatures of the night
While the moon is still grey
There will be more victims
When the dusk begins to decay

We must find her soon, I fear
Before it really is too late
Slow poison from her lips
Will drip and burn
Our deaths are all most certain

A painful memory will twist
The curls of her mouth
My name will be scrawled
In evil's ink for centuries
There is no more I can tell

Blood Lust

Most love the daylight
I embrace the night
I am the strongest creature
I have ever known
Bite by bite

These steely gray eyes
Search the kingdom
To hunt mortal prey
Under the frosty moon
Eternity's slave

A dark and gloomy soul
I am handsome, ancient
Brave, and dressed in black
And silken garb

I find it quite a thrill
When monsters
Move in for the kill
Then I really can't keep still

That's what makes this vampire grin
Make no mistake
I move closer to your throat
And so I want to taste your blood
My sacrificial goat

Pry open the casket
Hold out your arm
In your dreams and nightmares
I will do no harm
A crimson mess
Where the answer is always yes

Your blood is like wine
And just for tonight, House Red is just fine
I guess I have a really addictive personality
My dear, sweet succulent angel
I have smeared you with the blood of the many

Since your death, my desire for you only increases
I wish to feed on each other exclusively
"It was love," I sighed through razor-sharp teeth
Now I am truly frightened of what I have done
My soul is truly damned destined to roam
For an eternity alone

Wrapped in satin black, your body haunts mine
And your raven hair like soft moss drives me wild
Your crimson lips taunt me to feed
And now I believe I am becoming weak
For I loved a mortal with blue eyes

So stake me like the vampire that I am
Because of what could never be
This heart is dead
These veins run cold
Put me in the sun, and set me free
Because I am no longer the same old me

Darkest Possession

Ghouls and ghosts fill us with fright
As we sit alone
Under skeletal trees
Where winds scream defeat
Into dismal night
Here are the horrors
That haunt our past

In the air is a chill
That stirs the blood
A strong shadow approaches
Bending the weak light
of night around

In the temper of the monster's mind
I am defenceless as I totter to the ground
Breath like steely knives pierces my neck
I struggle to resist his dangerous grip
But in deepest dying I feel the vampire's kiss

Darkness shoots across the sky
And once or twice we heard him cry
What shape has come to us
With mouth so sweet and poisonous
And tortured hands so pale
Eyes so red and blind

Yet the strong heart loves me so
As the wind grows chill and cold

He comforts me with his love
And spellbound I hold my breath
With frozen lips in this living death

"His eyes have feasted on the dead
And dark and sinister his mouth," they said
As blood in moonlight is."
With whisperings and wails of pain
Silence falls again and again

Unholy Hungers

You were burning like fire
With stars in your eyes
Growling like black thunder
Before the deadly battle
With fangs shining
Avenger of the dark

Your lips bled with syrupy scarlet
On pillows stained in blood
As you sank your lips into
Unwilling flesh
Like the rosy snow in a wild dawn
Makes of a mist

On the edge of town
In this ancient graveyard
Clutching a cross in naked hand
Nowhere to hide in a forsaken land

You preyed on the lonely
Making us think we were
Your one and only
Leaving behind holes
Where you sucked out souls

Beg me to put you in the sun
And set you free
Pleasure will never be yours
As your soul purpose is to feed

Eternity calls forth the blood
Of breathless tears

Emotional vampire
There is no cure
For only seeking another's pleasure
Only the moon will remember
The hold you had on us throughout the years
In the winds of time, how blinded
Are we to our fears

She'll take you down slow
You won't even know
Until she releases her hold
Leaving behind only holes
Where she's sucked out your soul

She's an emotional vampire
She'll burn you like Hell's fire
A boiling cauldron spilling over
Like a dark cupid Witch
Hell's dark Pope
In evil's cradle
A Demon's kiss

She sparkles like a sapphire
That emotional vampire
She stalks the night
For what she can't put just right
A dark perpetual romance
In the glaring daylight

The Haunting

The lamplight was fading
As she fastened up her boots
The carriage was waiting
As she prepared for her rendezvous

The man had hair
The darkest black
His physique was slender
His name was Jack

They met at a dimly lit cafe
Where they would not be seen
Somewhere they'd never been
She nervously lit a cigarette
And ordered a drink that was wet

Their eyes locked, and they embraced
He kissed her face and then her neck
He suggested they leave at once
But she felt shy and uneasy
And felt in her purse for her loaded gun
The lanes were silent for miles around
Until all heard the screaming abound

Jack swore to avenge his fate
One shot to the temple
Yet it was too late

Rowena walked into the night
She chased the shadows

And cowered in fright
Looking in the bathroom mirror
At the blood that ran dry
She saw his face suddenly grimace in her eyes
Jack, in spirit, was very much alive

He goes where she goes,
In her tortured soul
Bones exposed at the fingertips
She waits for him every night alone

Jack sings to the silence
Burning up time
You cannot survive without me
Let me in, the cries
Is that the demon or her
Echoing throughout her head?

The lava lamp gives light
Her eyes slowly close
Hold me, I am home
Please don’t leave me here alone
I, too, Jack, am dead and cold

Reawaken the sleepers
And the murdered person
How do they sleep?
Awaken the heartbeat

Deadly Voices

Dead head, boneless
Under a flat stone
Breathing without dreams
Black blood to blame
The devil ate it once
In a murderous air
My new face is on
Now speak of her
The invention of a lie
Hooked by fakery
I cannot touch
A terrible truth
Ugly inside
Dismal and unsafe
Breeding like flies
Voiceless and new
I may be back

The Black Rose

A dark fog moves
Threateningly across the night sky
Lost without love
And our knights in armor
How they rust in a blighted eye
Did you fall from heavenly
Dreams for this black
Rose to find her way home?
Or are you without light to
Become a star?

We crawl back into the past
Battering and imprisoning us
You have no enemies you say?
I do not have time
For the 12th of never
My tears are like an evil flower
Succumbing to madness
Until I am nobody's darling

Break that knot again
You enthrall
Devil's flesh and bone
Does my shivering presence
Frighten thee like a shadow
On the wall?
Will I be weeping long?
To that infinite smile
I saw a thorn crying for
The dawn

Love's Goodbye

The universe was in your eyes
Where there was a world unborn
Your face was in every flower
Angel, and so thy thoughts
As thou art gone
The sky opened up
Whispering love's farewell
I whisper to you as the sea
Love shall slumber on
In your gaze at this hour
You are crowned as the sun
Even as I wrestle alone in
Solitude without you, dear
The shadow of our sorrows
Shall reach you from the stars
You'll feel it from the Heavens
It shall heal the scars
When sweet violets sicken
And the rose is dead
Your lovely star shall shine
I love you still even in death
And although a million tears I cried
We shall reunite at the end
And every sweet memory will
Bring you back to me time after time

A Poem for Two Voices

One can't go through life
Wishing and rubbing lamps
In the hopes of one last chance
The story goes on without me
It's a fallen world
I cringe with every footstep
And close my eyes in self-defence
Holding up one palm
I taste the summer and the solitude
I chase the stench of dying dreams
Night eats day like a ravenous wolf
Turning me into one of its ghosts
Now is the time I miss my
Calico-cat most
All is quiet, all is cold
I walk alone until the
Sun no longer shines

Angelus Mortis

The angel of death stands between
Earth and heaven with a drawn sword,
Gently transporting the soul to heaven,
Hurling the soul back down to earth.
Angel, Azrael with your many wings,

A body formed by as many eyes and
Tongues as there are living beings, of
Cosmic size, you stand with one foot
In the seventh heaven,

The other on the razor-sharp precipice
Of a bridge that divides Paradise and
Hell, bearing wings of snow and fire.
Brave angel who once faced the devil
On earth to help God create man,

With dominion over us at the
Crossroads of time, when we
Perish like a far-reaching spell,
The curse upon the land will
Burn like an earth inferno.

In this furnace, my voice is adorned
With glory and gloom, and the heart,
An anchor will rise above the shores
In a dreaming land.

Until the day God draws my soul out
Of the body, through His kiss, I shall
Spring over the wall of Paradise with
The angel's shining blade way up high
Beyond stars,

Light spills into the night
Under icy winter skies, a
Hunger once scorched is
Satisfied.

Though it did not sound like
Weeping, even still I call His name
That I would wake from another
Dream. Swaying in darkness, like
A shadow I do not crack,

O' Sun of the Morning, save one from
The dark and cold on your golden wings.
Angel, welcome me home by God's decree
With dancing and weeping so that I may
Glow like the soft light of a candle,

Under the cruel vault of night, a
Poet who sang and died with hands
Of fire, let me meet my destiny far
From the stench of fear, sweat, and
Blood,

Where only agonizing gods
Receive me into their arms,
Angel, Azrael, hear my prayer.
Do not take away my breath
Like a faint star,

Save me from a massacre of cruelty; the
Blood that is shed in the fountain of death.
Bear me up, Angel on the wings at dawn.
Enthrall my wandering heart, of dreams
And darkness. Come thou, my cloaked friend,
Where the dead cry out in ferocious anguish!

www.ingramcontent.com/pod-product-compliance
Lightning Source LLC
Chambersburg PA
CBHW050021170726
48282CB00025B/499
* 9 7 8 8 1 8 2 5 3 8 7 0 2 *